the
spring
garden

a seasonal guide to making the most of your garden

the spring garden

Richard Rosenfeld

LORENZ BOOKS

First published by Lorenz Books in 2002

© Anness Publishing Limited 2002

Lorenz Books is an imprint of Anness Publishing Limited
Hermes House, 88–89 Blackfriars Road, London SE1 8HA

Published in the USA by Lorenz Books, Anness Publishing Inc.
27 West 20th Street, New York, NY 10011

www.lorenzbooks.com

This edition distributed in Canada by Raincoast Books
9050 Shaughnessy Street, Vancouver, British Columbia V6P 6E5

A CIP catalogue record for this book is available from the British
Library.

Publisher: Joanna Lorenz
Managing Editor: Judith Simons
Design Manager: Clare Reynolds
Senior Editor: Doreen Palamartschuk
Additional text: Kathy Brown, Andrew Mikolajski and
    Peter McHoy
Editorial Reader: Penelope Goodare
Designer: WhiteLight
Photographers: Jonathan Buckley, Michelle Garrett, Sarah Cuttle
    and Peter Anderson
Indexer: Hilary Bird
Production Controller: Joanna King

10 9 8 7 6 5 4 3 2 1

page 1 *Crocus chrysanthus* 'Blue Pearl' is the perfect choice for
borders and containers.
page 2 *Crocus* 'Large Dutch Purple' plays a pivotal role in the
spring garden, providing a carpet of bright colour to contrast
with the early dwarf daffodils.
page 3 *Tulipa* 'Ballerina', a lily-flowered hybrid, is one of the most
striking of all tulips.
pages 4–5 *Tulipa* 'Striped Bellona' looks spectacular with bright
red wallflowers.

CONTENTS

INTRODUCTION

Spring is one of the busiest and most exciting seasons in the garden. After months of inactivity, with rain and cold temperatures, spring growth suddenly accelerates. The major new colour is lime green as the lawn puts on new growth, and the shrubs and trees explode in thousands of buds. Daffodils emerge, then tulips that can be as subtle or extrovert as you like, followed by the exotically beautiful magnolias, and rhododendrons that can be as high as a house. Getting the garden off to a smart start could not be simpler. The following pages are full of ideas that are sure to bring plenty of variety and colour into your garden.

left *Hyacinthus orientalis* 'Pink Pearl' is a spring favourite for its scent and colour. The pairing with the two-tone blue and white pansy, *Viola* 'Universal Marina', is highly effective.

THE BEST WAY TO PLAN A SPRING GARDEN, and see just what can be achieved, is to visit some beautiful public gardens and be inspired by them. Your own designs can easily be scaled down and modified. Don't just plan a spring garden around a handful of daffodils; be sure to include some sensational shapes and colours and you will have a sensory extravaganza.

large-scale mixed planting

With planning, you can create superb floral displays. If you have a spare patch of garden, or a long stretch of path, try creating a fantastic show of spring colour. Plant a row of lime trees down the centre, add decorative large pots and urns, and then begin underplanting the limes with hundreds of bulbs and perennials in a bright jamboree of red, white, blue and yellow.

right *Muscari armeniacum* will flower for many weeks from early to mid-spring. It combines well with tulips and violas.

above right *Tulipa* 'Queen of Night' is a striking, tall-growing variety, excellent for cutting. It flowers in late spring.

Go for a mix of scillas and daffodils, tulips and anemones, primroses with pulmonarias, and fritillarias with euphorbias, and the effect will be absolutely spectacular. When you see something on that scale, and with that much verve, you realize just how startling a spring show of flowers can be.

Once the main spring show has been planned, it is easy to work back to the late winter and early spring plants, and forward to the late spring and early summer flowers. There are scores of late winter performers, and the best include the tiny *Cyclamen persicum* and *Iris danfordiae*, and shrubs like *Camellia* 'Inspiration' that will flower in late winter if it is warm.

The many late spring flowers provide a good link to the start of summer. There is a much larger choice

of these plants, and they include the showy yellow laburnums, and clematis. With the ingredients in place, all you need do is sit back and enjoy.

creating a display

It is vital, when planning a spring display, that you check the different flowering times of the bulbs and the surrounding plants. There are tulips, for example, that flower in early, mid- and late spring. If the planning gets too complicated, go for just one big show in mid-season, which offers a wonderfully extensive and showy range of tulips.

If you have never grown tulips, get hold of a specialist bulb catalogue. Tulip colours range from whites, yellows and reds (soft and brash), to subtle purples and lilacs. Others come in twin colours, including startling yellow

with red stripes like 'Flaming Parrot', and the equally startling 'Frisbee', which has white cupped flowers ringed around the rim in red.

Use plants to help focus attention on the key features, like statues, splendid large urns or imaginative, topiarized shapes. When working out where to put each colour, it is an enormous help to plan the scheme by standing at key vantage points. This immediately helps clarify which colours you need in the foreground, the middle, and far distance.

Spring is a good time to create something new, whether it is a small tub or a large, multi-coloured border. The section in the book on garden styles gives ideas on how to make the best of the springtime plants. There are also many jobs to do and the essential tasks are covered – follow this advice for a successful and well-maintained garden.

above These *Narcissus cyclamineus* 'Jetfire', with their swept-back petals, look beautiful contrasted with an underplanting of *Crocus tommasinianus* 'Ruby Giant'.

SPRING PLANTS

The key to good gardening is a design that keeps the whole scheme alive, year after year, with beauty and panache, using supplementary plants to add a wide range of features. You need tiny plants for underplanting and small spaces, large shrubs to add impact, flowers for colour and scent, and surprises like the climbing *Akebia quinata* with its brownish-purple flowers. The following plant gallery, divided into bulbs, annuals, perennials, shrubs, climbers and trees, has enough high-quality, top-grade plants to turn any garden into an excellent spring showpiece.

left *Tulipa* 'Blue Parrot' in a massed bedding display with *Aubrieta* 'Royal Red'.

bulbs

Not all the plants that are called bulbs are true bulbs; some are actually corms, tubers or rhizomes. But they are all equally easy to plant and grow. It is best to buy and plant them the moment they are available, choosing fresh, firm, healthy stock. Avoid any bulbs that have come into premature growth by putting out green shoots, or which are soft, hollow or blemished.

The planting depths for bulbs will vary, and the best guide is the size of the bulb. Dig a hole that is twice the length of the bulb when the soil is on the heavy side, and three times its length when it is lighter and more free-draining.

After flowering, leave the foliage to die down naturally. This takes about six weeks, or four with smaller bulbs like crocuses. During this time the plant stores energy for next season's display. If the bulbs' foliage is cut too soon, next season's display will be adversely affected. When the bulbs are growing in a lawn, it will mean you have to wait until they have died down before mowing the grass in that area.

below left to right
Chionodoxa luciliae, Anemone blanda and *Crocus sieberi* subsp. *sublimis* 'Tricolor'.

Anemone blanda

Commonly known as the windflower, anemones are solitary flowers, about 2.5cm (1in) or more across. They have 10 to 15 white, pale blue or dark blue, sometimes mauve and pink petals. The attractive leaves are fern-like. They associate beautifully with primroses and all early dwarf daffodils, and are excellent in garden borders, beneath a tree or in pots. They form lovely, spreading flower clumps.
Flowering height 10–15cm (4–6in)
Flowering time Late winter to early spring, over 6 to 8 weeks
Hardiness Fully hardy

Camassia leichtlinii subsp. *leichtlinii*

This camassia is also known as the Indian lily and bears tall racemes, 10–30cm (4–12in) long, of star-shaped, creamy white or blue flowers, each 5–7.5cm (2–3in) across. It associates well with *Narcissus poeticus* var. *recurvus* (pheasant's eye narcissus).
Flowering height 75cm (30in)
Flowering time Late spring to early summer
Hardiness Frost hardy

Chionodoxa luciliae

This will naturalize in borders or beneath trees. It has up to 3 star-shaped, blue flowers, 1–2cm ($\frac{1}{2}$–$\frac{3}{4}$in) wide and with white centres, are borne in racemes.
Flowering height 15cm (6in)
Flowering time Early to mid-spring
Hardiness Fully hardy

Crocus sieberi subsp. sublimis 'Tricolor'

A beautiful spring plant. Each petal has three bands of colour: yellow at the centre, white, then blue-purple.
Flowering height 5–7.5cm (2–3in)
Flowering time Late winter to early spring
Hardiness Fully hardy

Cyclamen persicum

The pink, red or white flowers have darker staining towards the mouth, and the heart-shaped leaves are often patterned. Many cultivars have been bred, and there are various shades and sizes to choose from, but look for those with a sweet scent and attractively marked foliage. Among the many florist's cyclamens are the scented, miniature Miracle Series.

Flowering height 10–20cm (4–8in)
Flowering time Early winter to early spring
Hardiness Frost tender

Erythronium dens-canis

A pretty spring flower, dog's tooth violet has dainty, swept-back petals that may be white, pink or lilac, and prominent anthers. The leaves have blue and green markings. Plant in borders or among short fine grasses.
Flowering height 10–15cm (4–6in)
Flowering time Spring
Hardiness Fully hardy

Fritillaria imperialis

An impressive flower, often known as the crown imperial, it produces a stout stem topped by impressive umbels of 3 to 6 pendent bells, which may be orange, yellow or, more often, red, out of which a crown of glossy, leaf-like bracts emerges. Both the bulbs and flowers have a distinctive foxy smell.
Flowering height 70cm (28in)
Flowering time Late spring
Hardiness Fully hardy

above *Fritillaria imperialis.*

below left to right
Cyclamen persicum, Camassia leichtlinii subsp. *leichtlinii* and *Erythronium dens-canis.*

above *Hyacinthus orientalis* 'Amethyst'.

below left to right
Hyacinthus orientalis 'Jan Bos', *H. orientalis* 'Blue Jacket' and *H. orientalis* 'Hollyhock'.

Hyacinthoides non-scripta

The English bluebell bears single blue, sometimes white, flowers in graceful racemes, which bend over at the tip. Up to 12 pendent, narrow, bell-shaped, scented flowers are borne on one side only. Ideal for naturalizing beneath orchard trees. The pretty white form is known as *H. non-scripta* 'Alba'.
Flowering height 20–40cm (8–16in)
Flowering time Spring
Hardiness Fully hardy

Hyacinthus

Commonly known as the hyacinth, this is one of the most fragrant of all spring-flowering bulbs.

H. orientalis 'Amethyst'

Racemes of up to 40 single, lilac-amethyst, waxy, tubular, bell-shaped flowers, which are richly scented and are borne on stout, leafless stems.
Flowering height 20cm (8in)
Flowering time Spring outdoors (earlier indoors)
Hardiness Fully hardy

H. orientalis 'Blue Jacket'

The scented racemes of up to 40 single, dark blue, waxy, tubular, bell-shaped flowers make a good display.
Flowering height 20cm (8in)
Flowering time Spring outdoors (earlier indoors)
Hardiness Fully hardy

H. orientalis 'Hollyhock'

The double, crimson-red, tubular, bell-shaped flowers are richly scented and are borne on stout, leafless stems. 'Hollyhock' will combine beautifully with blue polyanthus primroses or perhaps with *Tanacetum parthenium* 'Aureum' (golden feverfew).
Flowering height 20cm (8in)
Flowering time Spring outdoors (earlier indoors)
Hardiness Fully hardy

H. orientalis 'Jan Bos'

The racemes have up to 40 single, cerise-red, tubular, bell-shaped flowers, which are scented and excellent with violas or primroses.
Flowering height 20cm (8in)
Flowering time Spring outdoors (earlier indoors)
Hardiness Fully hardy

Iris

This is a large genus of winter-, spring- and summer-flowering bulbs, rhizomes and fleshy rooted perennials.

I. danfordiae

A Reticulata iris with scented, lemon-yellow flowers, 5cm (2in) across which have green markings. They can be grown in the garden or in small pots.
Flowering height 10cm (4in)
Flowering time Late winter to early spring
Hardiness Fully hardy

I. 'Purple Sensation'

The purple-blue and bronze-yellow flowers of this Dutch iris are 7.5–10cm (3–4in) across. They work well under an arch of laburnum or wisteria and make excellent cut flowers. They also look very good near a pond, or planted around a pillar or statue.

Flowering height 45cm (18in)
Flowering time Late spring to early summer
Hardiness Fully hardy

Muscari

The genus, known by the common name of grape hyacinth, embraces 30 species of bulbs from the Mediterranean to south-western Asia. The best known is *Muscari armeniacum*, whose cultivars are pretty and very useful in borders, grassland and all sizes of containers.

M. armeniacum

Dense racemes of blue flowers are borne in bunches at the top of the stem. The exquisite colouring and long flowering make up for any waywardness of the foliage. Several cultivars are available, including double, soft blue 'Blue Spike' which, at 15cm (6in), is vigorous but slightly shorter than the species.

Flowering height 20cm (8in)
Flowering time Early to mid-spring
Hardiness Fully hardy

M. botryoides 'Album'

This muscari has slender racemes of scented white flowers. It is daintier than *M. armeniacum*.

Flowering height 15–20cm (6–8in)
Flowering time Early to mid-spring
Hardiness Fully hardy

above left to right *Iris danfordiae, Hyacinthoides non-scripta* 'Alba' (English bluebell) and *Muscari botryoides* 'Album'.

below left to right *Iris* 'Purple Sensation', *Muscari armeniacum* 'Blue Spike' and *Hyacinthoides non-scripta*.

Narcissus

Often known as the daffodil, this is one of the best loved of all bulbs, and the genus includes about 50 species that grow in a variety of habitats in Europe and northern Africa.

N. 'Actaea'

The pure white flowers have a brilliant scarlet eye. This is a delightful narcissus for borders or grasslands, and is an exceptionally good naturalizer.

Flowering height 45cm (18in)
Flowering time Mid-spring
Hardiness Fully hardy

N. bulbocodium

The hoop-petticoat daffodil, as this species is known, looks different from other narcissi. Allow it to naturalize on damp grassy slopes that dry out in summer.

Flowering height 10–15cm (4–6in)
Flowering time Mid-spring
Hardiness Fully hardy

N. 'Carlton'

This is a soft yellow daffodil with a large cup, which is frilly at the mouth. An excellent naturalizer, it is a delightful daffodil for borders or grassland.

Flowering height 45cm (18in)
Flowering time Mid-spring
Hardiness Fully hardy

N. cyclamineus

The golden flower has a distinctive shape with its sharply swept-back petals and long, narrow cup.

Flowering height 15–20cm (6–8in)
Flowering time Early spring
Hardiness Fully hardy

N. 'February Gold'

This is one of the best of all the early dwarf daffodils, elegant, long in flower, sturdy, short and useful in so many different parts of the garden.

Flowering height 25cm (10in)
Flowering time Early spring
Hardiness Fully hardy

N. papyraceus

Formerly known as N. 'Paper White', this daffodil bears bunches of 5 to 10 fragrant, white flowers.

Flowering height 40cm (16in)
Flowering time Spring, or winter indoors
Hardiness Frost hardy

N. 'Pipit'

Perhaps 2 to 3 exquisite two-toned flowers, each with a white cup and lemon-yellow petals, are borne on each stem. The flowers are sweetly scented.

Flowering height 30cm (12in)
Flowering time Mid- to late spring outdoors
Hardiness Fully hardy

N. 'Rip van Winkle'

This is a good choice for growing in short grass, at the front of borders or in small containers. It has striking double yellow flowers.

Flowering height 15cm (6in)
Flowering time Early spring
Hardiness Fully hardy

N. 'Suzy'

Clusters of 1 to 4 yellow flowers with flattened orange cups are borne on each stem. It is bred from fragrant N. jonquilla and inherits its strong perfume.

Flowering height 40cm (16in)
Flowering time Mid-spring
Hardiness Fully hardy

N. 'Thalia'

One of the taller dwarf daffodils, this has wonderful white flowers, often 2 or more to a stem.

Flowering height 30cm (12in)
Flowering time Mid-spring
Hardiness Fully hardy

above Narcissus papyraceus.

**opposite left to right
top row** Narcissus 'Pipit', N. cyclamineus and N. 'Carlton', **middle row** N. bulbocodium, N. 'Actaea' and N. 'February Gold', **bottom row** N. 'Rip van Winkle', N. 'Suzy' and N. 'Thalia'.

Tulipa

Tulips come in all shapes and sizes, with the smallest miniature kind growing about 10cm (4in) high, and the tallest tulip being about 60cm (2ft) high. Dig them up when they have died down, and store the bulbs in a dry airy place over summer for replanting in late autumn.

early spring tulips

Every spring garden needs some tulips. They provide fantastic flashes of colour, from soft hues to brasher, eye-catching combinations. Scores are single-coloured but hundreds have two colours.

T. 'Corona'

This hybrid is sometimes called a water-lily tulip. The long buds, often cream flushed with pink, open into stars of oval petals that expose different colour combinations. Their small size makes them ideal for the rock garden and formal beds.

Flowering height 15–20cm (6–8in)
Flowering time Early spring
Hardiness Fully hardy

T. 'Madame Lefeber'

A Fosteriana hybrid, with large, brilliant scarlet flowers. This is also known as 'Red Emperor', and is one of the best early red tulips.
Flowering height 20–40cm (8–16in)
Flowering time Early to mid-spring
Hardiness Fully hardy

T. 'Peach Blossom'

A Double Early hybrid, this short, sturdy tulip bears large rose-pink flowers. In a border, it teams well with violas and bellis daisies and it is sensational when underplanted with grape hyacinths.
Flowering height 25cm (10in)
Flowering time Early to mid-spring
Hardiness Fully hardy

below left to right
Tulipa 'Corona', *T.* 'Madame Lefeber' and *T.* 'Peach Blossom'.

mid-spring tulips

There is a huge colour range of mid-season tulips and many are beautifully marked or shaded. They are ideal for bedding and make superb cut flowers. They bloom towards the end of mid- and into late spring.

T. 'Apeldoorn'

The large scarlet flowers retain their petals for a long period of time. This tulip looks beautiful with lime-green foliage.
Flowering height 55cm (22in)
Flowering time Mid- to late spring
Hardiness Fully hardy

T. 'Apricot Parrot'

Parrot tulips look like the clowns among tulips: showy and extrovert, big and attention-grabbing, with large, lacerated, wavy, crested petals in pale apricot-yellow, with a hint of white. It makes an excellent bold cut flower, and is well worth growing in the garden if a sheltered spot can be found as it is vulnerable to wind damage.
Flowering height 45–60cm (18–24in)
Flowering time Mid- to late spring
Hardiness Fully hardy

T. 'Ballerina'

This is one of the most striking of all tulips, with its scented, orange flowers. It is excellent planted with other orange flowers or plants with bronze foliage, or in containers underplanted with deep blue pansies.
Flowering height 55cm (22in)
Flowering time Mid-spring
Hardiness Fully hardy

T. 'Plaisir'

This is vivid red outside, and vermilion inside, with lemon-yellow edges to the petals, and the foliage is beautifully mottled. Being a low grower, 'Plaisir' is suitable for pots and containers and the rock garden, as well as for formal bedding schemes.
Flowering height 15–30cm (6–12in)
Flowering time Mid-spring
Hardiness Fully hardy

T. 'Striped Bellona'

This has stunning cup-shaped, striped red and yellow flowers that will make a big impact in the garden.
Flowering height 50cm (20in)
Flowering time Mid-spring
Hardiness Fully hardy

above left to right *Tulipa* 'Apricot Parrot', *T.* 'Striped Bellona', *T.* 'Plaisir' and *T.* 'Ballerina'.

below *Tulipa* 'Apeldoorn'.

late spring tulips

Late-flowering tulips are among the most exciting, both in colour and shape.

T. 'Ballade'

These are distinctive and the tall wiry stems add to the impression of elegance. The large, open flowers are suitable for late spring bedding in sheltered areas, and also make superb cut flowers.

Flowering height 45–60cm (18–24in)
Flowering time Late spring
Hardiness Fully hardy

T. 'Blue Parrot'

A Parrot tulip, with single, large, lilac-blue flowers, and irregular crimping along the edge of the petals. It is exciting when in bud and when the flowers begin to unfurl. In borders it can be planted with pink or blue forget-me-nots, while in containers pink, lavender or violet-blue pansies are perfect.

Flowering height 60cm (24in)
Flowering time Late spring
Hardiness Fully hardy

T. 'Hamilton'

A bright golden-yellow tulip with petals that are edged with a conspicuous fringe. It is stunning in a border or makes excellent cut flowers.

Flowering height 45–60cm (18–24in)
Flowering time Late spring
Hardiness Fully hardy

T. 'Marilyn'

A bold Lily-flowered tulip, with large, open flowers like colourful stars. They are white with red stripes and a feathering of red at the base.

Flowering height 45–60cm (18–24in)
Flowering time Late spring
Hardiness Fully hardy

T. 'West Point'

This striking Lily-flowered hybrid has distinctive primrose-yellow flowers that look especially charming underplanted with blue forget-me-nots.

Flowering height 50cm (20in)
Flowering time Late spring
Hardiness Fully hardy

opposite *Tulipa* 'Marilyn'.

below left to right *Tulipa* 'Hamilton', *T.* 'Blue Parrot' and *T.* 'West Point'.

annuals

An annual is a plant that completes its life cycle within one growing season: the seed germinates, grows, flowers, sets seed and dies all within the space of a year. The seed is dormant until the return of conditions favourable to germination, usually the next spring. Biennials are similar, but take two years to complete their life cycle, usually flowering in the second year.

Annuals are unrivalled for bringing colour into the garden throughout the warmer months. They bring any border to life within a matter of weeks, and give new gardens instant style and impact. They can be used in all sizes and kinds of gardens and even in tubs, window boxes, hanging baskets and all types of containers. Many plants bring other rewards, being deliciously scented or attractive to beneficial insects, and some will provide an excellent source of cut flowers for the home.

top A deep purple *Viola* 'Penny'.

above *Viola odorata* (sweet violet) and *Primula vulgaris*.

Antirrhinum

The unique "snapping" lips of the flowers of snapdragons give them a certain appeal to children. These half-hardy annuals provide strong blocks of colour – white, yellow, orange, pink, and red (some flowers being bi-coloured) – in beds and borders. *Antirrhinum majus* Wedding Bells series and *A. majus* 'Coronette' are good late spring bedding plants. *A. majus* 'Black Prince' has deep crimson and bronze foliage.
Flowering height 45cm (18in)
Flowering time Late spring
Hardiness Half-hardy

Bellis perennis

The genus includes the pretty lawn daisies that generally appear unannounced in all gardens. This species is the parent of a number of seed strains, all producing rosettes of leaves and flowers in shades of red, pink or white. They are delightful in window boxes and are good bedding plants. 'Dresden China', a dwarf form, has small, pink, double flowers with

quilled petals. The Habanera series cultivars bear pink, white or red, long-petalled flowerheads. Cultivars of both the Pomponette and Tasso series bear double pink, white or red flowerheads with quilled petals – the Pomponette varieties are up to 4cm (1½ in) across, Tasso up to 6cm (2½ in).
Flowering height 10cm (4in)
Flowering time Late spring
Hardiness Fully hardy

Lunaria annua

Honesty is an erect fast-growing, modest annual or biennial that has two seasons of interest. The pretty spring flowers are followed by distinctive, papery, oval seedheads that are excellent in dried arrangements. *Lunaria annua*, a European species, usually has purple, sometimes white, flowers in spring followed by translucent white seedheads in autumn. For white flowers only, sow seeds of *L. annua* var. *albiflora*. 'Alba Variegata' is a desirable garden form with pointed-oval, serrated, white-variegated leaves and white flowers. 'Variegata' has similar leaves but with small scented flowers in shades of purple-pink.
Flowering height 1m (3ft)
Flowering time Late spring
Hardiness Fully hardy

Myosotis sylvatica

The species has mid-blue, yellow-eyed flowers in spring and early summer and grey-green leaves. Although forget-me-nots will seed on their own freely, it is worth sowing these plants afresh every season – the named forms always have flowers of a more intense colour than their natural progeny. Indispensable for most spring bedding schemes, forget-me-nots make a classic cottage-garden combination with tulips. 'Blue Ball' is a more compact form with indigo flowers. The flowers of 'Compindi', another dwarf form, are even darker. 'Rosylva' is something of a novelty, with clear pink flowers.
Flowering height 30cm (12in)
Flowering time Spring
Hardiness Fully hardy

Viola

This endearing genus includes a delicate wild form known as heartsease, as well as rock garden plants, perennial sweet-scented violets, and the well-known pansies. Some are self-coloured, but many are attractively bi- or even tri-coloured with mask-like markings that make the flowers look like faces.
Flowering height Up to 23cm (9in)
Flowering time Late spring
Hardiness Half-hardy

above left to right *Bellis perennis* 'Tasso Rose', 'Tasso Red' and 'Tasso White', *Antihirrhinum majus* 'Black Prince', *Viola tricolor* and *Lunaria annua*.

opposite bottom *Myosotis* (forget-me-nots) are excellent spring bedding plants, and help to fill in the space around the long-stalks of *Tulipa* 'Warbler'.

perennials

For many, a spring garden just would not be the same without the contribution of perennials, often long-lived plants that provide interest year on year. They encompass many early-flowering plants (usually low-growing) that are delightful with spring bulbs and are good in herbaceous borders. If you have a perennial that you like, you can easily take cuttings in the summer, providing extra, free plants. Generally, a young, 10cm (4in) long, non-flowering shoot gives the best results.

Anemone

This large genus includes some excellent perennials. Their late season and tolerance make them essential plants for any garden. The flowers are carried on tall, elegant, wiry stems. They are ravishing in drifts under deciduous trees, or they can be used in borders.

A. nemorosa

Commonly known as the wood anemone, these plants bear dainty, demure, solitary white flowers, sometimes with a pink flush.

Flowering height 7.5–15cm (3–6in)
Flowering time Late spring
Hardiness Fully hardy

A. ranunculoides

The yellow wood anemone has rich yellow flowers. Though low growing, reaching 10cm (4in) high at most, it spreads well and makes a beautiful show.
Flowering height 5–10cm (2–4in)
Flowering time Mid-spring
Hardiness Fully hardy

Convallaria majalis

With flowers of instantly recognizable fragrance, lily-of-the-valley is a deservedly popular cottage-garden plant. This species spreads by means of branching underground rhizomes. The handsome leaves emerge in spring and are followed in late spring by elegant sprays of bell-shaped, fragrant white flowers. The plants can also be potted up and forced under glass for early flowers. All are toxic.
Flowering height 23cm (9in)
Flowering time Mid- to late spring
Hardiness Fully hardy

Dicentra formosa

Easy plants to grow, dicentras have ferny foliage and elegant, arching stems. They are excellent in shady rock gardens or light woodland, but they also tolerate more open conditions, combining well with cottage-garden plants, such as aquilegias, flowering around the same time in late spring. *D. formosa* var. *alba* is the desirable white form.

Flowering height 45cm (18in)
Flowering time Late spring to early summer
Hardiness Fully hardy

Erysimum

Wallflowers and tulips are a classic cottage garden combination. The plants described here are all true evergreen perennials, and although they are often short-lived, cuttings easily increase them. All are of hybrid origin.

E. 'Bowles' Mauve'

This perennial belongs in every garden. Officially it produces its four-petalled, fragrant, rich mauve flowers from late winter to early summer, but it is seldom without flowers at any time of year.

Flowering height Up to 75cm (30in)
Flowering time Mid- to late spring
Hardiness Fully hardy

Euphorbia polychroma

The true flowers of euphorbia are insignificant, but are surrounded by showy bracts (referred to as 'flowers') that continue to attract attention after the true flowers have faded. All are easy to grow, but care needs to be taken when handling them: when cut or broken, the stems exude a milky sap that can cause skin irritations, particularly in bright sunshine. Always wear a good pair of gardening gloves. *E. polychroma* is a must for the spring garden, making a mound of foliage that in late spring becomes a mass of brilliant yellow-green as the flowers open.

Flowering height 30cm (12in)
Flowering time Mid-spring to midsummer
Hardiness Fully hardy

Helleborus foetidus

Hellebores have nodding flowers and handsome, more or less evergreen leaves. All are poisonous, but handling them will not produce any problems. *H. foetidus* (stinking hellebore) makes a clump of blackish-green leaves. Strong stems carrying many bell-shaped, apple-green flowers appear from late winter to early spring. It looks good with snowdrops.

Flowering height 75cm (30in)
Flowering time Into early spring
Hardiness Fully hardy

above *Erysimum* 'Bowles Mauve'.

below left to right
*Dicentra formosa,
Convallaria majalis* and
Euphorbia polychroma.

Primula

This large and complex genus, which includes the well-known primroses, contains about 400 species of perennials, some suitable for mixed plantings, others for bedding, while a few are happiest in a rock garden.

The plants that are described here do well in cool, damp atmospheres and moisture-retentive, preferably neutral soil. All have characteristic rosettes of spoon-shaped leaves from which the flowering stems arise. Another characteristic (but not of all) is 'farina', a flour-like bloom on the stems and leaves that can provoke an allergic reaction.

Shorter growing primulas are delightful with dwarf spring bulbs and are good in window boxes. Primroses and polyanthus are archetypal cottage-garden plants, while moisture-lovers are effective near water, preferably the running water of a stream. Primroses are among the few plants that combine happily with rhododendrons, as well as being good companions for the smaller hostas. So-called Candelabra types are distinctive and graceful plants, with flowers carried in whorls up the stems, and need rich, moist soil.

opposite *Primula beesiana.*

below left to right *Primula japonica, P. japonica 'Miller's Crimson' and P. vulgaris.*

P. beesiana

This Candelabra primula, which is deciduous or semi-evergreen, produces whorls of cerise-pink flowers in tiers on long, sturdy stems.
Flowering height 60cm (2ft)
Flowering time Late spring to early summer
Hardiness Fully hardy

P. japonica

In moist, shady places in Japan, this pretty, deciduous primula thrives and produces red-purple to white Candelabra-type flowers.
Flowering height 45cm (18in)
Flowering time Mid-spring
Hardiness Fully hardy

P. veris

The evergreen or semi-evergreen yellow-flowered cowslip is a familiar sight in damp meadows. It can be established in grass, as long as the ground is moist.
Flowering height 25cm (10in)
Flowering time Late spring
Hardiness Fully hardy

shrubs

Shrubs encompass a wide range, from tree-like plants (which can substitute for trees in small gardens) to more diminutive ones that can be used in rock gardens or as ground cover. Most are grown for their often-spectacular flowers, but others have less obvious attractions – showy berries or good leaf colour or an appealing habit. Judiciously chosen, shrubs give an air of permanence to any planting.

Camellia

This is a large genus, containing about 250 species of superb evergreen shrubs and small trees, made larger by the number of hybrids. Unfortunately for many gardens they must have acid soil, but, they thrive in containers where you can provide suitable conditions. Use camellias as specimens in large tubs or barrels in courtyards or patios, or in shrub borders. All camellias have lustrous green leaves, making them splendid backdrops to other plants when they have finished flowering.

below left to right
Camellia 'Elizabeth Hawkins', *Ceanothus* 'Dark Star' and *Camellia* 'Jury's Yellow'.

C. 'Elizabeth Hawkins'

A cultivar of *C. japonica*. It has anemone-form, bright pinkish-red flowers.
Height 2m (6ft)
Flowering time Mid-spring
Hardiness Fully hardy

C. 'Inspiration'

A reliable, upright plant (verging on a small tree) that has semi-double, deep pink flowers. This is good when trained as a wall shrub.
Height 4m (13ft)
Flowering time Midwinter to late spring
Hardiness Fully hardy

C. 'Jury's Yellow'

One of the *C. x williamsii* hybrids. The slow-growing 'Jury's Yellow' has anemone- to peony-like flowers, with creamy-white outer petals and creamy-yellow inner ones. This is the nearest to a yellow camellia.
Height 2.5m (8ft)
Flowering time Mid- to late spring
Hardiness Fully hardy

Ceanothus

The Californian lilac is highly prized for its show of true blue, deliciously scented flowers. There are deciduous and evergreen species, the evergreens being slightly more tender. In cold areas all are best grown in the shelter of a sunny wall, but in warmer climates they make truly spectacular specimens. The pink- and white-flowered types are of interest but less popular.

C. 'Dark Star'

Dark purplish-blue flowers are carried in spring on this arching evergreen.
Height 2m (6ft)
Flowering time Late spring
Hardiness Half-hardy

C. 'Delight'

This evergreen variety, which has clusters of rich blue flowers, makes a good wall shrub.
Height 3m (10ft)
Flowering time Late spring
Hardiness Half-hardy

Choisya ternata

Mexican orange blossom is a handsome evergreen with glossy green leaves and a neat, rounded habit. It flowers mostly in spring with, often, a second flush in late summer or autumn. The leaves are highly aromatic. Choisyas tolerate some shade and are good growing against a wall.
Height 2.4m (8ft)
Flowering time Spring
Hardiness Fully hardy

Daphne

Evergreen, semi-evergreen or deciduous, these shrubs bear flowers with an exquisite fragrance. Some are rock garden plants, but most thrive in borders. Winter-flowering types are best sited near a door where their fragrance can be appreciated to the full, without the need to go too far outdoors. *D. tangutica* is a small, evergreen species with fragrant white flowers comes from China.
Height 1m (3ft)
Flowering time Late spring
Hardiness Fully hardy

above left to right
Daphne tangutica, Camellia 'Inspiration' and *Choisya ternata*.

below *Ceanothus* 'Delight'.

Pieris

These elegant evergreen woodland shrubs bear racemes of lily-of-the-valley-like flowers in spring.

P. 'Forest Flame'

The flush of leafy growth in spring is brilliant red.

Height 2.2m (7ft)

Flowering time Mid- to late spring

Hardiness Borderline hardy

P. japonica

Lily-of-the-valley bush has glossy green leaves and cascading sprays of white flowers in spring. Good forms include 'Pink Delight', 'Valley Rose' and the prolific 'Valley Valentine'.

Height 3m (10ft)

Flowering time Late winter to spring

Hardiness Fully hardy

Rhododendron

This large genus includes plants that range from huge, tree-like shrubs to diminutive specimens for a rock garden or alpine trough. All need acid soil.

R. 'Bruce Brechtbill'

This has a dense habit and pale pink flowers.

Height 2m (6ft)

Flowering time Late spring to early summer

Hardiness Fully hardy

R. 'Cary Ann'

A compact shrub with coral pink flowers that is good for small gardens.

Height 1.5m (5ft)

Flowering time Late spring to early summer

Hardiness Fully hardy

R. 'Chanticleer'

A spectacular plant that produces a rich display of maroon-purple flowers.

Height 1.5m (5ft)

Flowering time Late spring to early summer

Hardiness Fully hardy

R. 'Grace Seabrook'

A robust and vigorous form bearing conical trusses of deep pink, often reddish flowers.

Height 2m (6ft)

Flowering time Early to mid-spring

Hardiness Fully hardy

Viburnum carlesii

This deciduous species from Japan and Korea is almost unmatched for the scent of its white spring flowers, pink in bud and carried in rounded clusters. 'Diana' has purplish-pink flowers that fade to white.

Height 1.5m (5ft)

Flowering time Spring

Hardiness Fully hardy

opposite, clockwise from top left Rhododendron 'Bruce Brechtbill', Pieris 'Forest Flame', Rhododendron 'Cary Ann' and Pieris japonica.

above left to right Rhododendron 'Chanticleer', Viburnum carlesii 'Diana' and Rhododendron 'Grace Seabrook'.

climbers

These are among the most dramatic and rewarding garden plants, lifting your eyes skywards as they reach towards the sun. They are ideal for beautifying walls, fences and ugly outbuildings, and can also be draped over pergolas to provide welcome shade, or used to carpet banks. Some have spectacular flowers that emerge in spring and can be deliciously scented. Others are grown for their leaves, while the evergreens provide year-round interest.

Clematis

There is a clematis for virtually every season of the year. All the following, group 1, flower during the spring on the previous year's growth. Prune the bushes after flowering.

C. armandii

This species, one of the few evergreen clematis, has long, leathery, dark green leaves and clusters of scented, white flowers in spring. A vigorous plant, it is best trained against a warm wall in cold areas. 'Apple Blossom' is pale pink.
Height 3m (10ft)
Flowering time Early spring
Hardiness Borderline hardy

C. cirrhosa

This is usually the first clematis to flower and typically it begins to bloom in midwinter, but some flowers can be produced as early as autumn. These are bell-shaped, with a papery texture, and are creamy-white in colour, sometimes speckled with brownish-red inside.
Height 3m (10ft)
Flowering time Late winter to early spring
Hardiness Borderline hardy

C. macropetala

The bell-shaped flowers of this species, which appear in mid- to late spring, have only four petals, but appear to be double because some of the stamens are petal-like. They are blue or violet-blue. 'Blue Bird' has semi-double, clear blue flowers. The charming 'White Moth' (syn. *C. alpina* 'White Moth') has pure white flowers.
Height 3m (10ft)
Flowering time Spring to early summer
Hardiness Fully hardy

C. montana

The most vigorous of the early clematis, this is the last to flower. Species include 'Continuity', with creamy-white, pink-tinged flowers; 'Elizabeth', which has pale pink, richly scented flowers; and the vigorous *C. montana* f. *grandiflora*, with white flowers.

below left to right *Wisteria sinensis, Clematis macropetala with buds of C. montana, C. montana* 'Continuity' *and Wisteria floribunda.*

Height 6m (20ft)
Flowering time Late spring and early summer
Hardiness Fully hardy

Wisteria

Possibly the most desirable of all flowering climbers, wisterias bear dramatic racemes of scented pea flowers from late spring to early summer. Old specimens trained against house walls are breath-taking, as are those trained to embrace arching bridges over water. They are also spectacular growing over arches, pergolas or – in a less formal garden – allowed to ramp into sturdy host trees. When buying wisterias, look for named varieties grafted on to vigorous rootstocks, expensive though these are.

W. floribunda

The Japanese wisterias are slightly shorter than the Chinese kind, but have equally long racemes of scented flowers. In a warm spell they will appear in late spring, otherwise slightly later. Good forms include 'Multijuga' whose racemes of light blue flowers can reach 1m (3ft) long. 'Alba' has white flowers. 'Violacea Plena' has double flowers verging on purple.

Height 9m (30ft)
Flowering time Late spring and early summer
Hardiness Fully hardy

W. sinensis

The Chinese wisterias tend to be more vigorous than the Japanese kind. The species has faintly-scented, violet-blue flowers that appear in 20–30cm (8–12in) long racemes before the leaves. Two other good forms worth growing are the white-flowering 'Alba', and 'Caroline' with slightly larger, rich blue-purple flowers. 'Prolific' lives up to its name, and produces a superb show of flowers that will not let you down.

Height 15m (50ft)
Flowering time Late spring and early summer
Hardiness Fully hardy

above *C. montana* 'Elizabeth'

below A beautiful well-established wisteria in full bloom covering the front of a house.

trees

A tree completes a garden. Whether it is grown for its flowers, fruits, foliage or overall appearance, a tree adds dignity and style to any garden. From oaks to the more manageable Japanese maples, there is a tree for every type of garden whether you have rolling acres or a suburban plot. Even if you have only a courtyard, balcony or roof garden, there are trees suitable for containers. Careful selection is necessary, as a tree often outlives the gardener.

Acacia dealbata

Mimosa or silver wattle is a pretty evergreen Australian and Tasmanian species with silver-grey, fern-like leaves and masses of fragrant, fluffy yellow flowers from late winter to early spring. It is suitable for training against a sunny, warm sheltered wall.
Height 15m (50ft)
Flowering time Early spring
Hardiness Half-hardy

Cercis siliquastrum

The unusual Judas tree, native to south-eastern Europe and south-western Asia, is quick-growing and produces dark pink flowers on the bare wood in spring. The kidney-shaped, blue-green leaves turn yellow in autumn. The tree can be trained against a wall. The shrubby form *C. siliquastrum* f. *albida* has white flowers and pale green leaves.
Height 10m (33ft)
Flowering time Mid-spring
Hardiness Fully hardy

below left A smart combination with a magnolia tree underplanted with grape hyacinths.

below right *Acacia dealbata.*

Magnolia

Sumptuous and stately, magnolias are among the most handsome of garden trees, as well as being among the hardiest. Drawbacks of some of the species are their enormous size, slowness of growth and reluctance to flower until some 20 or more years after planting. Fortunately, most of the modern selections are free from these vices. The deciduous spring-flowerers make excellent features.

M. campbellii

The large, cup-and-saucer-shaped flowers, to 30cm (12in) across, are either white or pink.
Height 15m (50ft)
Flowering time Late winter to early spring
Hardiness Fully hardy

M. 'Pickard's Schmetterling'

A spreading tree, this bears goblet-shaped, rich pinkish-purple flowers. The flowers open as the leaves emerge.
Height 10m (33ft)
Flowering time Mid-spring
Hardiness Fully hardy

M. stellata

Star magnolia is a slow-growing, deciduous species. It is indispensable in a spring garden with masses of beautiful, spidery white flowers. It requires a sheltered spot.
Height 1.2m (4ft)
Flowering time Mid-spring
Hardiness Fully hardy

Malus 'John Downie'

As well as a plethora of fruit-bearing trees, this genus includes a number of trees of ornamental value that suit cottage-style gardens. M. 'John Downie' is one of the finest crab apples, and the best for making jelly. The cup-shaped, white flowers are followed by quantities of egg-shaped, orange and red fruits.
Height 6m (20ft)
Flowering time Late spring
Hardiness Fully hardy

Prunus 'Hillieri'

There are a huge number of ornamental cherry trees. A cherry orchard is a spectacular sight when in flower, and an ornamental cherry should be among the first choices for a flowering specimen. P. 'Hillieri' is a spreading tree with clusters of soft pink flowers. P. x cistena has pink flowers with purple centres.
Height 10m (33ft)
Flowering time Mid-spring
Hardiness Fully hardy

Sorbus aria 'Lutescens'

This form of whitebeam is more compact than the species, and so is better suited to medium gardens. The leaves are covered in creamy-white hairs and are brilliant as they emerge in the spring. The heads of white flowers that appear in late spring are followed by red berries. Another good choice is S. aria 'Majestica'.
Height 10m (33ft)
Flowering time Late spring
Hardiness Fully hardy

above left to right
Magnolia campbellii, Sorbus aria 'Lutescens', Prunus x cistena and *Magnolia 'Pickard's Schmetterling'*.

below *Prunus x subhirtella.*

SPRING DISPLAYS

There are so many different styles of gardening, whether your taste is for a Mediterranean look, a rampant, half-wild cottage garden, or a highly formal design with neat, ordered beds. Whatever form of garden you choose, you can highlight spring plants in a host of exciting ways in beds, borders, or around a pond or water feature. There are also all kinds of unusual pots and tubs for patios and window boxes to make great displays.

left This mixed spring border includes bold groups of daffodils, red and yellow tulips and wallflowers edged with blue primroses.

planting out

Bulbs and spring-flowering plants such as primroses can be planted in many ways, for example, in beds and borders, under trees and in lawns.

naturalization

Most gardens have a patch of lawn, even if they are not very big, providing a chance to plant bulbs in what is called the 'natural way'. This means, quite simply, letting the bulbs grow through the grass, and this is especially effective around the base of deciduous trees. The canopy of leaves will not yet have emerged, which means that sunlight and moisture will still be able to reach the ground beneath the crown. The area can then be filled with just one sort of bulb such as *Narcissus* 'February Gold' or a massed planting of, say, scillas or chionodoxas. Once planted, you can leave them to take care of themselves for years on end, and the effect, without fail, works every time. They will multiply freely, only needing occasional dividing if they become too congested.

   When planting the bulbs, make sure you allow plenty of space for them to spread. The best way to

above right *Crocus vernus* naturalized in grass.

right *Narcissus* 'February Gold' is one of the best of the early dwarf daffodils. Lustrous in colour, it is early to flower, sturdy, long lasting and elegant in shape. Planted en masse, it creates a generous flash of yellow beneath an old cherry tree.

far right
A bank of *Scilla bithynica* looks marvellous in the dappled light beneath a broad deciduous tree.

achieve a natural, non-contrived look is to take a handful of bulbs and freely scatter them on the ground, then plant them where they fall. To plant in a lawn, you can either dig individual holes for each bulb or pull back a strip of lawn for several bulbs. The former involves using a trowel, or a bulb planter that pulls out a plug of earth. Fork up and loosen the base of the hole, pop in the bulb and cover. When removing a strip of lawn, slice through the ground with a spade on three sides of a square, and then roll it back. In both cases it is absolutely vital that you use vigorous, quick spreading bulbs such as *Crocus tommasinianus* that can compete with the tough grass. If the grass is quite fine, then you should have no problems using less vigorous bulbs. You can cheat and get a longer show of naturalized flowers by planting several bulbs at a slightly deeper depth than normal.

colourful ideas

Use fresh yellow in spring, but do not overdo it. There is a wide range of other colours. For example, scented hyacinths come in white, blue, pink and crimson, primroses in just about every shade you can think of, and daffodils in white, pink, orange and marmalade. Keep schemes lively and varied.

It is also vital that the colour schemes, no matter how beautiful, combine well with the adjoining arrangement. A sensational foreground show of gentle pinks will immediately lose its impact if planted under a cherry tree with a great aerial display of pink blossom. Choosing the right colour means being able to set it off against colours that will highlight your planting scheme and not diminish it.

For strength and warmth of colour, plant the brighter, richer-coloured tulips and grape hyacinths among vibrant red, orange or blue polyanthus primroses or amid the blues and purples of violas and pansies. Plan the borders in autumn and reap the rewards in spring. The results will be well worth the care taken over planning.

above *Tulipa* 'Orange Nassau' is a vibrant orange-red and associates well with red polyanthus. You could also include *Tanacetum parthenium* 'Aureum' (golden feverfew) or bright green herbaceous plants.

left Try planting two kinds of bulbs together. Here *Scilla sibirica* has been planted between 'Pink Pearl' hyacinths.

below Tulips and blue camassias are used lavishly in this border of shrubs and herbaceous plants.

right Daffodils and anemones contrast wonderfully together.

opposite Bright spring flowering borders with large groups of *Tulipa* 'Christmas Marvel'.

beds and borders

If your garden does not hit a full colourful stride until early summer, it needs a large injection of spring-flowering performers. This means either spring bedding (one-season plants subsequently removed to make way for summer annuals, for example), or more permanent plants. The big problem, when digging planting holes, is remembering exactly where other plants are deep down in the ground. The last thing you want when digging a hole is to hear a sound like a speared potato as your fork plunges into an allium bulb.

One good way round the problem is to plant bulbs that enjoy light shade under and around shrubs, where nothing else is growing. Then, when the bulbs die down in early summer, the shrubs take over. You can mark other planting positions the previous summer, when you can see what is growing where, by placing bricks or stones where you want the planting holes. It might look odd for a while, but it is only for a few months. This also helps clarify exactly how many spring plants you have room for. Try to avoid sporadic, isolated shows of colour, and aim for lively spring combinations with at least two or three different kinds of plants with plenty of style. One classic combination is yellow tulips with blue forget-me-nots.

containers

There is one excellent reason for growing spring plants in containers. No matter how bad the weather, with late spring frosts and freezing conditions, you can keep the containers in the greenhouse, in relative warmth, ready for putting out when conditions improve. Do make sure that you gently acclimatize them to outside conditions first, though.

 Growing plants in containers also means that you can keep some plants indoors, in the warmth, forcing an early spring show instead of the one that would normally occur, say, at the end of the season. And the third and final benefit of growing spring plants or bulbs in containers is that you can highlight and position them exactly where you like, instead of having their positions dictated by the garden layout.

hanging baskets

You certainly get the biggest and showiest displays in the summer, but that does not mean that you cannot create some excellent spring displays.

 Begin by buying a large hanging basket, into which you can pack plenty of plants. Sit the basket firmly on a large pot or bucket, and then line the inside of the bottom half of the basket with one of the many types of liners available, such as sphagnum moss, and half fill with potting compost (soil mix). Then carefully insert the roots of the chosen plants from the outside, in. When the bottom half has been planted, firm in the root balls with more compost, and then add sphagnum around the top inner half of the basket. Continue planting up in this way.

 Excellent plants include trailing, small-leaved, variegated ivies to hang down, bright pansies around the sides, hyacinths and small, highly-scented narcissi

left Blue *Muscari* (grape hyacinth) and red tulips blend beautifully together.

like Jonquils (especially when the hanging baskets are at head height so that you can smell them), tulips and wallflowers. For a smart vertical focal point, try a young thin conifer that can later be planted out in the garden. When hanging up the basket remember that after it has been watered it will be very heavy, and that strong 'fixings' are required to make sure it does not crash down.

right This gorgeous hanging basket is a stylish mixture of *Viola* 'Bowles Black', *V.* 'Johnny Jump Up' and *V.* x *wittrockiana* with Double Early tulips and *Muscari armeniacum* (grape hyacinth).

below *Bellis perennis* 'Tasso Red' and 'Tasso Rose', *Primula veris,* and violas give visual interest to this unusual edible hanging basket full of parsley, rosemary, eau-de-cologne mint, marjoram and golden lemon balm.

window boxes

You cannot beat a bright show of colours right outside your window. Unlike hanging baskets, which usually look better with an array of plants, boxes can be elegant and stylish with just one kind of plant. That can be a row of hyacinths, so that their scent can waft indoors on warm days when the window is open, or the smaller, elegant narcissi like *N. cyclamineus* 'Jack Snipe', with white petals and a yellow centre. The effect can be enormously improved by placing shapely pebbles and stones on the soil surface. You can even go one better by painting the window box a contrasting colour, for example rich blue or slate grey, or for something slightly livelier try dark red with thin yellow, curving wispy lines.

top left A small metal window box planted with narcissi is perfect for a kitchen windowsill or for the conservatory.

top right Window boxes in subdued, natural wood are the perfect foil for a vibrant display of colourful spring flowers

right An eye-catching window box with *Narcissus* 'Hawera', *Viola* 'Sunbeam' and *V.* 'White Perfection' set off by the silver-grey foliage of *Senecio cineraria*.

tubs, pots and scent

If you have a spare patch of patio or terrace, it is well worth patterning it with a smart range of tubs and pots so that they are almost as eye-catching as the plants. Aim for a variety of styles from large, impressive urns down to smaller, old-fashioned pots for crocuses.

The bigger pots need strong, dominant plants. They might include tender plants that were moved under cover over winter, like the fantastically dramatic *Agave americana* with its long, stiff, fleshy pointed leaves that can grow 2m (6ft) long. At this time of year it needs a warm, sheltered spot, and a quick dash into the conservatory if there is a sudden frost.

Camellias are far less demanding, especially the smaller hardy ones like the beautiful C. 'Nicky Crisp'. It flowers from early to mid-spring, has pink flowers, and will not exceed 1.5m (5ft).

For one of the strongest scents in the spring garden you need *Daphne odora* 'Aureomarginata'. The pale pink flowers open in early spring. You will get the most from this slow-growing shrub, which will reach about 1.2m (4ft) high, by placing it in a sunny, windless corner.

above *Hippeastrum* 'Red Velvet' gives a reliable spring show of colour.

above left *Tulipa* 'Blue Heron' and orange wallflowers make a vibrant combination. The gentle scent from the wallflowers is an added bonus.

above left A spring triumph of glorious soft pink tulips and early-flowering pansies in shades of blue.

above centre Tulips planted with forget-me-nots are a classic combination.

above right A pretty container full of *Viola odorata, Primula vulgaris* and golden feverfew plants.

right Dwarf irises, crocuses and primroses brighten up a warm day in early spring.

ceramic pots

Ceramic or clay pots really stand out in the spring garden before the summer flowers start hogging the limelight. A huge array of decorative ceramic pots are available with ornamental features, including Italian and Greek style, and they need a prominent position. They also need clever, imaginative planting that will not let them down.

Some of the most intriguing spring plants include the fritillarias. *Fritillaria imperialis* (crown imperial) grow about 1.5m (5ft) high, and need big bold pots. The stems have plenty of leaves lower down, with a bare stretch above, and right at the top stunning, downward-pointing yellow, orange or red flowers.

Far smaller, but almost as startling, are the 50cm (20in) high red and yellow tulips, *Tulipa acuminata*. They need 45cm (18in) wide pots, and a light background that will show off their spidery thin petals, 10cm (4in) long, yellow at the base and bright red towards the tip. They add an exotic touch. But even without such plants, most displays look good in ceramic. It adds immediate style.

other containers

It is all too easy to limit oneself when buying pots, by sticking to the tried and tested such as clay and plastic. You can use all kinds of containers such as old wooden barrels, provided they have drainage holes in the bottom. It does not even matter if your containers are flimsy, like old boots and shoes, they may only last one season, but they will make an eye-catching display.

Look around architectural salvage yards and rummage sales for fun, unusual containers. Lead or other metal ones often have patterns on the outside, and if you build up a special collection the patterns could be highlighted and arranged up a flight of steps.

Given a lightly shaded position, they look marvellous when planted with *Polygonatum* x *hybridum* (common Solomon's seal). The stems arch up and out, with dangling white flowers. You could even stand an old dresser, given a lick of paint, firmly fixed in position outside against a wall, putting a collection of unusual pots on the shelves. You can then line up old rubber boots filled with compost and daffodils, in front.

above left The delicate heads of *Primula veris* look charming alongside the pretty blue *Viola* 'Penny', planted up together in a rustic basket that would be ideal in a cottage garden.

above right The teapot is planted with violas and *Narcissus* 'Hawera', which is a neat little daffodil with a multitude of dainty lemon-yellow flowers.

right *Convallaria majalis* (lily-of-the-valley) in a metal tub from an architectural salvage yard.

spring styles

It does not matter what kind of garden style you have, whether it is smart and modern, stark and minimalist or wonderfully old-fashioned, there is always room for a strong display of spring plants. The secret is choosing the most suitable plants for your preferred style, and then finding the right position. The former is quite easy, but the latter can be incredibly tricky. Many gardeners find themselves moving plants two or three times before they are in the right position. Thereafter they should quickly flourish.

the formal style

Gardens in formal style have strong, clearly defined, regular shapes, and the plants have clearly fixed positions. Chaotic jungles they are not. When planting out bulbs like tulips, for example, aim for large, solid displays with equal spacing between each bulb. Impressive order is the keynote.

above right Subtle and cool interplanting with the lovely *Tulipa* 'Spring Green' and white bellis daisies.

right A mixed spring border includes red and yellow *Tulipa* 'Striped Bellona'.

far right Spring-flowering bedding plants such as forget-me-nots, bellis and winter flowering pansies have been used extensively in this garden to fill in between the bulbs. These plants also help to extend the period of colour, as they bloom for a long period.

left Spring in a cottage garden bed with an abundant planting of primulas, forget-me-nots, columbines and bluebells.

below A camellia planted with *Viburnum tinus* and *Elaeagnus* makes an effective backdrop to spring-flowering perennials.

romantic ramblers

Cottage gardens have a loose, free-flowing design, with hazy boundaries between the different areas. The plants are encouraged to self-seed, ramble, and climb like clematis. While tall plants generally go to the back, and the small to the front, the rule need not always be followed.

It adds enormous and quirky fun to have the likes of three *Fritillaria imperialis* (crown imperial) shooting up beside a path, or even the back door, the flowers grow on stems that are 1.5m (5ft) high. For a low-down effect there is *Fritillaria meleagris* (snake's head fritillary), 30cm (12in) high, that will make a mosaic of pinkish-purple bells, provided the soil never dries out. Or try bulbous Juno irises that need dry, well-drained ground. The easiest to grow are the lilac *I. cycloglossa* and white to lemon-yellow *I. bucharica*. Reliable Bearded irises add a lovely floppy show of petals, and for a weird and wonderful effect go for *Arisaema griffithii*, which starts poking out of the ground in the spring like a snake. For a moist, shady site there is *Erythronium dens-canis* (dog's tooth violet) with its delicate, spiky petals. A yellow forsythia sets off the whole scene.

bold designs

Contemporary gardens make good use of modern structures, gadgets and clean, simple paving. They use painted decking, outdoor lighting, architectural plants, jets of water rather than traditional fountains, and can look like an upbeat, outdoor room. Plants can either be used to soften or accentuate the look.

Softening spring plants include blue scillas, *Anemone blanda* with starry blue, white or pink flowers, and deep blue *Chionodoxa sardensis*, with plenty of white snowdrops (*Galanthus nivalis*). Spanish bluebells (*Hyacinthoides hispanica*) give a better show than the English kind. And if you want just one or two quite beautiful flowering shrubs to set off the hard landscaping, *Rosa mutabilis* is one of the first roses to flower in spring, in a warm, sheltered site, and ends with flourishes in the autumn. The buds are flame red, with light pink flowers that darken with age.

right A strikingly unusual water feature, surrounded by a glorious mid- to late spring border of fluffy spikes of *Smilacina racemosa* (false spikenard).

below A deep blue wooden centrepiece filled with grasses is the focus of this modern patio area. Bright marigolds in the borders add colour and contrast in late spring.

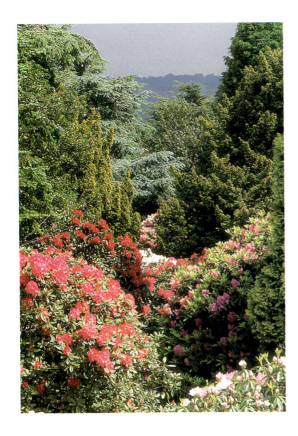

sunny styles

Drought-tolerant plants are the key plants for a Mediterranean look, with pots, strong scent and bright colours. A vertical rosemary can be pruned to add shapeliness – try 'Miss Jessopp's Upright', or the upright 'Tuscan Blue'. With its dark blue spring flowers, it will catch the eye, especially when underplanted with small, bright red species tulips like *Tulipa linifolia*. Blue aubrieta on white walls also gives a terrific, early season contrast.

flamboyant planting

Decorative leaves, rich colours, interesting shapes and tender plants make up the exotic garden. Top of any shopping list is a cherry tree for its sensational spring blossom and a *Gunnera manicata* (given a large patch of damp soil) for its new spring growth of sharply-toothed leaves that grow like satellite dishes to 2.5m (8ft) high. You also need a *Magnolia stellata* (star magnolia) with its pretty white flowers. Add a bamboo and *Iris reticulata*, and the picture is complete.

above left Lush, richly colourful rhododendrons.

above A collection of pots with bright grape hyacinths create a Mediterranean feel.

water gardens

right Moisture-loving plants, such as ferns and candelabra primulas, create an almost tropical atmosphere around this informal pool.

below A naturalistic waterfall nestling within a rock garden contrasts with the smooth, semicircular slate paving and the fresh green foliage and yellow spring flowers.

Ponds slowly revive in the spring as the water starts to warm up. For a wide range of wildlife do not add fish because they will eat anything small that moves, especially tadpoles. With luck newts will move in. The young frogs and newts like a still, shallow, sheltered patch of water where they can safely mature, usually amongst the emerging shoots of irises. There are two kinds of irises for wet ground, those that like bog gardens (*Iris ensata* and *I. sibirica*) and those for shallow water (*I. laevigata*, *I. pseudacorus* and *I. versicolor*). All are excellent.

Pond water tends to be on the green side for a few weeks, until the oxygenating plants come to life.

A plant that looks good and helps keep the water clear is *Stratiotes aloides* (water soldier). It looks like the leaves on a pineapple. The spring-flowering *Hottonia palustris* (water violet) is also very effective. Both grow in deep water. For more spring flowers, try planting the yellow *Caltha palustris* (kingcup) and *Myosotis scorpioides* (water forget-me-not). The last two like the shallow water around the edge of a pond.

above A sheltering rustic woven fence and a wood-decked seating area add a country feel to this densely planted pond surrounded by primroses, irises and soft spring colours.

right Bold blue irises soften the harsh lines of the decorative metal grille covering this pool. The grille serves as a safety feature and keeps feeding herons away from the fish.

SPRING TASKS

Spring is one of the most enjoyable times in the garden. It means preparing the soil in the borders and vegetable garden, sowing seeds of annuals, herbs, fruit and vegetables, and most important of all, making sure that all the new emerging seedlings are not slaughtered by hungry pigeons and hordes of slugs and snails. Get everything right now, and you will have great flowering displays in just a few weeks.

left The exquisite lily-flowered *Tulipa* 'West Point' vies for attention with red and yellow polyanthus, all bordered with dark blue forget-me-not, *Mysotis sylvatica* 'Music'.

above Traditionally, perennials are bought bare-rooted, having been grown in the ground and dug up when needed. Bare-rooted plants should be bought only between late autumn and early spring.

early spring

In cold regions the weather can still be icy in early spring, but in mild climates you can make a start on many outdoor jobs. If sowing or planting outdoors, bear in mind that soil temperature as well as air temperature is important. Few seeds will germinate if the soil temperature is below 7°C (45°F), so use a soil thermometer to check before you sow.

kitchen gardens

Warm soil, by day and night, is particularly important when sowing tender herbs like basil. Instead of sowing all your seed now and seeing only a few plants emerge, it is better to wait until the end of spring or early summer when germination rates will be higher.

If you have cloches then use them like blankets to warm up the soil before sowing vegetables like lettuce. Otherwise, you can start sowing lettuces in small pots or buckets indoors. This gets the plants off to a racing start. Gradually harden them off, standing them outside in a sheltered place or in a cold frame, until they can be planted out. The added benefit is that being larger they are less likely to be shredded by the early morning birds. Tasty new crops should be covered by nets to keep pigeons away, and beer traps

right Buying annuals in strips is a popular method of obtaining large numbers of plants at low cost. Young plants have plenty of room to develop a good root system.

above When planting new herbaceous plants, make sure the ground is weed-free and start at the rear of the border.

the flower garden

❖ Finish planting bare-root trees and shrubs
❖ Plant container-grown shrubs
❖ Plant herbaceous plants
❖ Sow hardy annuals, like sweet peas
❖ Feed and mulch beds and borders
❖ Plant gladioli and other summer bulbs
❖ Start mowing the lawn, but cut high initially; reduce the height of the blades thereafter
❖ Sow a new lawn or lay a lawn from turf
❖ Recut or neaten edges of the lawn
❖ Buy seeds and bulbs if not already done so
❖ Prune shrubs, if necessary
❖ Prune roses always making sure that you cut directly above a shoot
❖ Tidy up the rock garden, and apply fresh stone chippings where necessary
❖ Clean out the pond, and make sure that there are no rotting leaves at the bottom
❖ Add scatterings of pelleted poultry manure on flower beds

above Cut out any diseased or damaged wood back to sound wood, just above a strong bud.

will reduce the slug numbers. Place the traps away from the new crops and not amongst them, or the slugs will reach the crops before drowning.

beds and borders

One of the biggest bugbears of gardening is the amount of time spent watering over summer. The best way to avoid this is to wait until after a few days of heavy spring rain, when the soil is deeply saturated, and then spread a thick layer of mulch such as mushroom compost over the soil. This locks in the moisture now, and after subsequent waterings. It also keeps down weeds and helps condition the soil.

cutting lawns

The best way to keep a healthy green lawn is to give it a first light cut in the spring. Thereafter give it a medium cut, or the longest possible cut for your needs, such as children's games. The longer the grass the longer the roots, and this means it will stay lusher and greener for longer during dry spells. Lawns that are cut very short have short roots that cannot go deep down for moisture during long dry spells, and they are the first to go brown.

the greenhouse and conservatory

❖ Take chrysanthemum cuttings
❖ Start off begonia and gloxinia tubers
❖ Take pelargonium and fuchsia cuttings
❖ Take dahlia cuttings
❖ Sow seeds of bedding plants and pot plants
❖ Prick out or pot up seedlings sown earlier
❖ Increase ventilation on warm days
❖ Check plants for signs of pests and diseases, which often begin to multiply rapidly as the temperature rises
❖ Container-grown fuchsias need cutting back now and repotting
❖ Untie climbers so that you can repaint or clean the backing surface
❖ Buy new pots, and paint old ones in pastel and hothouse colours
❖ Thoroughly clean out the greenhouse, checking old pots for slugs and snails
❖ Sharpen secateurs

above Seedlings are almost always pricked out individually, but lobelia seedlings are so tiny that they should be pricked out in groups of five or six at a time.

below Plant an area of bedding before positioning the bulbs between the plants.

mid-spring

above Plant up containers for summer displays.

This is when the garden really comes alive, but while day-time temperatures can dramatically shoot up, beware sudden, crippling frosts. Also, keep seedlings ticking over on windowsills or in greenhouses, shading them on days when the sun is too fierce.

dahlias

Last year's dahlia tubers should now be sprouting new shoots. As they grow, make sure that they receive sufficient water and light. If it is too dark, the shoots will be weak and spindly. While dahlias are chiefly grown for their autumn colour, the established plants brought on early will add terrific colours from midsummer. New cuttings flower later.

weeding

One of the best reasons for doing the weeding yourself, and not hiring someone else, is that you will quickly start to know the difference between weeds

above Take cuttings from the tips of the stems and put them in a plastic bag. This keeps them safe and moist before planting.

the flower garden

❖ Plant container-grown shrubs
❖ Plant herbaceous plants
❖ Stake herbaceous and border plants
❖ Feed beds and borders
❖ Plant hedges
❖ Plant gladioli and other summer bulbs
❖ Plant ranunculus tubers
❖ Mow the lawn regularly from now on
❖ Make a new lawn from seed or turf
❖ Buy seeds and bulbs if not already done so
❖ Plant out sweet peas raised in pots
❖ Sow sweet peas where they are to flower
❖ Sow hardy annuals
❖ Take softwood cuttings
❖ Plant hanging baskets
❖ Water newly planted shrubs and trees in dry spells
❖ Start weeding in earnest
❖ Divide perennials

above When planting up a hanging basket, standing it on a pot or bucket helps to keep it stable.

and seedlings of plants that you want to keep. If the latter are growing in the wrong place, pot them up and grow them on for planting in the border later.

lawn care

This is a good time of year to level out any hollows in the lawn. The simplest way to tackle any small dips where people might trip over, is by half-filling the hollow with a good loam-based compost (soil mix). The grass will gradually grow up through it, and in from the side. Next month, fill the hollow to the top, and by midsummer the lawn should be firm and flat.

deadheading daffodils

The best way to guarantee a good show of daffodils for next year is to deadhead them, once they have finished flowering. Do not remove the foliage (that continues helping store energy) until nearly dead.

above right Remove the flowerheads of daffodils before the seed has time to develop.

above When replanting divided perennials, dig the soil over first, removing any weeds, and add some well-rotted organic manure.

above Work out where you want your shrubs before planting them, allowing room for them to fill out.

the greenhouse and conservatory

- ❖ If the greenhouse was not given a thorough spring-clean last month, now is your last chance
- ❖ Last year's dahlia tubers that are not putting out new shoots, need 18°C (65°F) and gentle watering
- ❖ Pot up or pot on into larger pots chrysanthemums rooted earlier
- ❖ Take leaf cuttings of saintpaulias and streptocarpus
- ❖ Reduce watering for winter-flowering cyclamen
- ❖ Pot up tomato seedlings into larger pots if necessary, or sow seed of greenhouse crops now
- ❖ Buy packets of plant labels
- ❖ Check new growth on pot plants for aphids
- ❖ Ventilate on warm days, but close shutters in the evening in case of night-time frosts
- ❖ Provide greenhouse shading to protect plants from high temperatures

above If you do not have a propagator, enclose cuttings in a plastic bag secured with a twist-tie.

above Plant up a herb pot for the summer. Unless the pot is very large, don't try to pack too many herbs into the top. It is better not to plant shrubby plants at the top.

late spring

Even late spring can be deceptive. It often seems as though summer has arrived, yet in cold areas there can still be severe late frosts. Take local climate into account before planting any frost-tender plants outdoors. Even with experience it can be a gamble as an untypical season might produce surprises. Judging when frosts are no longer likely is mainly a matter of assessing risk.

It is a good idea to watch when summer bedding is put out in the local parks. These gardeners will have amassed generations of local knowledge of your area, which is by far the best guide.

lemon trees

When buying potted lemon trees (actually shrubs, pruned to whatever size you want, unless you have the space to let them take off), keep them under glass for a while. They dislike a sudden change of temperature. Spray them regularly to provide

above Many plants will grow as a single stem, making spindly growth. If the tip is cut or pinched out, side shoots will develop and the plants will become more bushy.

above Half baskets are planted to look good from the front only and do not need to be turned as normal baskets.

the flower garden

❖ Plan visits to public gardens and flower shows
❖ Give formal hedges a light trim for shape and to encourage bushness
❖ Edge flower beds regularly to give a clean shape
❖ Give spring-flowering shrubs a light pruning
❖ Start standing houseplants outdoors when the weather is warm enough
❖ Remove the spring bedding and replace with a lively summer display
❖ Weed regularly in the vegetable garden
❖ Finish practical projects like new ponds
❖ Check that the new growth on climbers is tied in
❖ Seedlings of hardy annuals need thinning out
❖ Save reserve plants of courgettes (zucchini), etc., in case those planted out unexpectedly fail
❖ Check that there are no holes in the bird netting in the kitchen garden
❖ Cordon tomatoes need their side-shoots removing (this does not apply to outdoor bush tomatoes)
❖ Feed lawns and continue to mow regularly

above Marginal aquatics should have a lining around the container so that the soil does not fall through the sides.

humidity, and stand them out in a warm sheltered position next month. Removing the flower buds on young plants diverts the plant's energy into stem growth and leaves. After a couple of years, start to let it fruit.

ponds

As the water warms up, algae will proliferate. Selectively weed it out, leaving some for the tadpoles to hide and feed in. Meanwhile, introduce new plants into the pond, and provide larger containers for established plants where necessary.

border plants

To get new border plants off to a good start, dig a large planting hole and remove any weeds. Most plants also benefit from some well-rotted compost amongst their roots. By the time the whole garden has been planted out, all the beds should have been considerably enriched.

above Use a cloche when hardening off plants raised indoors or in a greenhouse.

above When planting a new shrub, check that the hole is deep enough by placing a stick or cane across it.

the greenhouse and conservatory

❖ Check that shading is in place
❖ Damp down greenhouses in hot spells by hosing the floor to add humidity
❖ Add adjoining water butts for a ready supply of rainwater
❖ Start creating special pot plant displays
❖ The early spring-sown bedding plants can be moved to a cold frame for hardening off
❖ Regularly clean out the greenhouse to prevent the build-up of pests
❖ Water well any plants grown in greenhouse beds
❖ Pot up plants, if roots protrude out of existing containers, to the next size pot
❖ Check that cordon tomatoes have a sturdy support (a cane or secured rope) to climb up

above Pink dicentras planted with forget-me-nots and pale yellow primroses.

notes

Through trial and error, you can create the garden of your dreams, with the certain knowledge that you will have another chance to get it right the following year. Use these pages to record your planting successes and failures.

annuals

Type ....

Variety ....

....

Sown ....

Thinned ....

Tip for next year ....

Type ....

Variety ....

....

Sown ....

Thinned ....

Tip for next year ....

bulbs

below *Tulipa* 'Color Cardinal'.

Type ....

Variety ....

....

Planted ....

Flowered ....

Tip for next year ....

Type ....

Variety ....

....

Planted ....

Flowered ....

Tip for next year ....

perennials

Type ....

Variety ....

....

Planted ....

Flowered ....

Tip for next year ....

Type ....

Variety ....

....

Planted ....

Flowered ....

Tip for next year ....

climbers

Type ....

Variety ....

....

Type ....

Variety ....

....

Pruned ....

Flowered ....

Tip for next year ....

Pruned ....

Flowered ....

Tip for next year ....

shrubs

Type ....

Variety ....

....

Type ....

Variety ....

....

Pruned ....

Flowered ....

Tip for next year ....

Pruned ....

Flowered ....

Tip for next year ....

herbs and vegetables

Type ....

Variety ....

....

....

Type ....

Variety ....

....

....

Sown ....

Thinned ....

Taste ....

Tip for next year ....

Sown ....

Thinned ....

Taste ....

Tip for next year ....

above Daffodils and bushy wallflowers provide a colourful spring display.

below *Rhododendron* 'Exbury White'.

index

Page numbers in italic refer to the illustrations

above *Camassia* with buttercups.